WHERE ARE WE?

A Biblical Perspective on the Timing
of the Rapture and Tribulation

JON REDEKOP

WHERE ARE WE?: A BIBLICAL PERSPECTIVE ON THE TIMING OF THE RAPTURE AND TRIBULATION
Copyright © 2025 by Jon Redekop

All rights reserved. Neither this publication nor any part of this publication may be reproduced or transmitted in any form or by any means, electronic or mechanical, including photocopying, recording or any information storage and retrieval system, without permission in writing from the author.

Unless otherwise indicated, scripture quotations are taken from the Holy Bible, NEW INTERNATIONAL VERSION®, NIV® Copyright © 1973, 1978, 1984, 2011 by Biblica, Inc.® Used by permission. All rights reserved worldwide. • Scripture quotations marked (NLT) are taken from the Holy Bible, New Living Translation, copyright © 1996, 2004, 2015 by Tyndale House Foundation. Used by permission of Tyndale House Publishers, Inc., Carol Stream, Illinois 60188. All rights reserved. • Scripture quotations marked (ESV) are taken from the ESV® Bible (The Holy Bible, English Standard Version®), © 2001 by Crossway, a publishing ministry of Good News Publishers. ESV Text Edition: 2025. The ESV text may not be quoted in any publication made available to the public by a Creative Commons license. The ESV may not be translated in whole or in part into any other language. Used by permission. All rights reserved. • Scripture quotations marked (NKJV) are taken from the New King James Version®. Copyright © 1982 by Thomas Nelson. Used by permission. All rights reserved. • Scripture quotations marked (NASB) are taken from the New American Standard Bible®, Copyright © 1960, 1971, 1977, 1995, 2020 by The Lockman Foundation. All rights reserved. • Scripture quotations marked (CSB) are taken from The Christian Standard Bible. Copyright © 2017 by Holman Bible Publishers. Used by permission. Christian Standard Bible®, and CSB® are federally registered trademarks of Holman Bible Publishers, all rights reserved. • Scripture quotations marked (YLT) are taken from the 1828 Young's Literal Translation of the Holy Bible, which is in the public domain. • Scripture quotations marked (KJV) are taken from the Holy Bible, King James Version, which is in the public domain.

ISBN: 978-1-4866-2717-2
ebook ISBN: 978-1-4866-2718-9

Word Alive Press
119 De Baets Street Winnipeg, MB R2J 3R9
www.wordalivepress.ca

Cataloguing in Publication information can be obtained from Library and Archives Canada.

CONTENTS

THE NAME. THE QUESTION.	v
INTRODUCTION QUESTION: WHEN WILL THE RAPTURE TAKE PLACE?	vii
ONE: SIGNS	1
TWO: SOMETHING DIFFERENT	5
THREE: IS THERE A RAPTURE?	17
FOUR: DIFFERENT ANSWERS	21
FIVE: THE SERIES—IS IT POSSIBLE TO KNOW WHEN THE RAPTURE WILL OCCUR?	25
SIX: WHEN WILL THE RAPTURE TAKE PLACE?	35
SEVEN: DOUBLE MEANING	43
EIGHT: TRACKING	45
NINE: DANIEL'S SEVENTY WEEKS	47
TEN: ASTEROID	49
ELEVEN: THE AFTER DATE	53
TWELVE: THE BEFORE DATE	67
THIRTEEN: AI	71
FOURTEEN: THE THIRD TEMPLE	73
FIFTEEN: FIFTY REASONS WHY THE RAPTURE IS CLOSE	75
AUTHORS NOTE	79
APPENDIX	81

THE NAME. THE QUESTION.

WHEN WE THINK of a calendar, we generally think of our one-year calendars. If God were to think of His calendar, He might think of eight thousand years. If you had a couple of seconds to see His calendar—a total start to finish earth calendar—what would you do? Would you ask the questions "Where are we?" or "How much time is left?" I've been researching these questions for quite some time, and the Lord has revealed many things to me. He's also allowed me to find some information on my own. If you find the topic of the Lord's calendar intriguing, this book is for you!

INTRODUCTION
QUESTION: WHEN WILL THE RAPTURE TAKE PLACE?

THERE ARE SO many ways to answer that. Two thousand years ago, Jesus told parables. If I were to share a parable today, it would go like this:

A father had three children. I ask you: At what time on what day will the child get his driver's licence? Some people would say this is a silly, impossible question. Some would ask who the father was, how old the child was, and where they're getting their licence. They'd get answers, but the answers would have nothing to do with the meaning of the parable. So what's the meaning of the parable? Can we find out the day and the hour? No. But that doesn't mean there's nothing to know. The real questions are: Are you interested in questions or are you interested in answers? How much do you want to know?

If it was possible to tell people in less than two minutes when the Rapture will occur, and leave them with a warm, fuzzy feeling, then I'd like to try. Many people think of Matthew 24:36, where Jesus says, *"no one knows the day or hour"* (NLT), referring to the events of the end times. Some people have gone further with that answer: If we don't know the day or the hour, it could be anytime. It could be two minutes from now, or two hundred years from now. But if you really do your research, you'll learn that the Bible doesn't support this.

WHERE ARE WE?

There are very few hints in Scripture regarding the timing of the Rapture, but there are many hints about the timing of the Tribulation. Let me give you one verse with one hint. *"Since you have kept my command to endure patiently, I will also keep you from the hour of trial that is going to come on the whole world to test the inhabitants of the earth"* (Revelation 3:10, NIV). In other words, "I will keep you from the hour of trial." From this verse, we learn that there will be a time of trial, and the Lord will keep us from that. This means that there will be a time of trial on earth and we won't be here. One theory about the timing of the Rapture is called Post-Trib, meaning it won't occur until after the Tribulation, but this verse clearly gives a different perspective.

Christians can go in a few different directions when considering theological or end-times questions. Two examples would be:

1. Those who don't know all that's in the Bible but have had Matthew 24:36 drilled into their heads have no interest in exploring the question further and are totally comfortable where they are. The problem with this, though, is that we're not supposed to live in just one verse: *"Man shall not live on bread alone, but on every word that comes from the mouth of God"* (Matthew 4:4).
2. Those who consider other verses, such as the following: *"Blessed is he that readeth, and they that hear the words of this prophecy, and keep those things which are written therein: for the time is at hand"* (Revelation 1:3, KJV); *"So then, let us not be like others, who are asleep, but let us be awake and sober"* (1 Thessalonians 5:6).

QUESTION: WHEN WILL THE RAPTURE TAKE PLACE?

I declare to you, brothers and sisters, that flesh and blood cannot inherit the kingdom of God, nor does the perishable inherit the imperishable. Listen, I tell you a mystery: We will not all sleep, but we will all be changed—in a flash, in the twinkling of an eye, at the last trumpet. For the trumpet will sound, the dead will be raised imperishable, and we will be changed. (1 Corinthians 15:50–52)

So that your daily life may win the respect of outsiders and so that you will not be dependent on anybody. Brothers and sisters, we do not want you to be uninformed about those who sleep in death, so that you do not grieve like the rest of mankind, who have no hope. 14 For we believe that Jesus died and rose again, and so we believe that God will bring with Jesus those who have fallen asleep in him. (1 Thessalonians 4:12–14)

There are many hints in the Bible, but do you want to know? This brings us to another question: Does God want us to know? Yes, but He leaves the choice to us, possibly with no punishment or discipline if we choose not to seek answers.

"For God has not destined us for wrath, but to obtain salvation through our Lord Jesus Christ, who died for us so that whether we are awake or asleep we might live with him" (1 Thessalonians 5:9–10, ESV). When reading and interpreting these verses, one must keep a couple of things in mind:

WHERE ARE WE?

1. These verses were written to people who were somewhat aware of what's written in the Scriptures.
2. When Moses was leading the children of Israel to the Promised Land, there was an incident with the rock. Moses was to speak to the rock, but he hit it instead and was punished for it.

Verse 9 of the passage above can be split into two parts. First, God doesn't want us to be on earth during the time of wrath. Second, He wants Christians in heaven during that time. This is what God desires for people as they live their lives.

Verse 10 can be split into four parts:

The first part explains the way of getting into heaven.

The second part asks us to reflect on if we're awake and aware of what's going on around us. Do we conduct research into where we are on God's calendar? Do we study the biblical end-time prophecies and relate them to what's happening in the world? Or do we fail to study the Bible and pay attention to what's happening in the world?

The third part deals with punishment for making the wrong decision. The punishment isn't mentioned, meaning it's our choice whether we're awake or asleep.

The fourth part wraps it up nicely. If you are a Christian, you get to go to heaven.

#
SIGNS

AS SOON AS you start talking about prophecy and the end times, someone asks when you think the Rapture will take place. It would be nice if God gave us a sign that said, "You should really start to think about getting ready." What if that sign was in the Bible? Do you know where to find it? Do you know how much time you have left until the date of the sign occurs?

"Nation will rise against nation, and kingdom against kingdom" (Matthew 24:7a). This can very easily be interpreted as what happened in World War One and World War Two. The First World War was fought from 1914 to 1918. That was more than one hundred years ago. How much notice did you want?

> A great sign appeared in heaven: a woman clothed with the sun, with the moon under her feet and a crown of twelve stars on her head. She was pregnant and cried out in pain as she was about to give birth. (Revelation 12:1–2)

In order to understand this great sign (some Bible versions title the passage "The Great Sign"), you should consider a few concepts from the last sign (the star of Bethlehem). Over two thousand years ago, a sign appeared in the sky, and it was known as the Bethlehem star. The Bible refers to the star as a sign, and the use of "a" means it could be one of many. The star was a sign pointing to the birth of Christ.

How many people knew of Jesus when He was born? How many understood the meaning of the Bethlehem star? The population of the world today is estimated to be around 8 billion people. At the time of Jesus's birth, it was around 300 million. The population of the Roman Empire at that time is estimated at 45 million, and the population of Jerusalem was around 40,000. The population of Bethlehem when Jesus was born is estimated at 300. How many shepherds were in the field? Maybe ten? The kings from the East had told Herod about the star, so some government officials knew, but they were trying to keep it a secret. So even if fifty people knew in comparison to the world population at that time, one could say it was a secret for a select few.

If you could only use ten words, what would you say was the most important part of Jesus's life: His many miracles, His death on the cross, the resurrection, or the ascension into heaven? Possibly you'd say His death on the cross, where He took on the sins of the world, and rising from the dead. If this is your answer, then the most important thing happened over thirty years after the sign of the star.

Jesus's impact on the world began when He was twelve years old and spent a couple of days in the temple teaching/talking to the elders. His parents were travelling home and unaware of where Jesus was. When they did find Him, Jesus said He needed to be in His Father's house. This event seemed to disturb Mary and Joseph, and it could be interpreted as a test to see how others would react to His teaching. The conclusion was that even if He was ready to

ONE: SIGNS

teach others, others weren't ready to receive His teaching, so He delayed His ministry until the world was ready to listen to Him. By that time, He was approximately thirty years old. Jesus's earthly ministry only lasted around three years.

If you're driving toward a main highway and come to rumble strips, red lights, and stop signs, where is the main event? At the stop signs? Or is the main event located after the stop signs? You now realize that you didn't pay attention to the side traffic.

Simply put, the star was sent as a sign for those who were interested enough to watch and search for something that was important in God's plan and would follow closely behind the sign.

In Revelation 12, we read about "the great Sign." In this context, "great" could mean that it's much bigger than any other sign; it could even be more important than the star of Bethlehem.

So when did the great sign of Revelation appear? You can Google this question or watch an informative video titled "How Rare Is the Revelation 12 Heavenly Sign [2017] once in 7000 Years."[1] In this video, September 23, 2017 is presented as a significant date, possibly the date of the appearance of "the sign."

Jesus said *"… you will not see me again until you say 'Blessed is he who comes in the name of the Lord'"* (Luke 13:35b). He said this specifically in Jerusalem, which can be interpreted as meaning that the Jews will be in Jerusalem. But the Jewish people scattered in AD 70, and have had to survive almost two thousand years with no homeland.

---

[1] Chisza7, "How Rare Is the Revelation 12 Heavenly Sign [2017] once in 7000 Years," YouTube video, October 19, 2014, 14:54, https://www.youtube.com/watch?v=XXxVw-pcXV0U.

WHERE ARE WE?

> ... This is what the Sovereign Lord says: I will take the Israelites out of the nations where they have gone. I will gather them from all around and bring them back into their own land. 22 I will make them one nation in the land, on the mountains of Israel. (Ezekiel 37:21–22a)

The Balfour Declaration of 1917 allowed the Jewish people to come back to Israel. By May 14, 1948, there were enough Jewish people in Israel that it was recognized as a nation, and in 1967, after the Six-Day War in Israel, facing unbelievable odds, the Jewish people captured Jerusalem.

But this might not be good enough for some people. What is needed is for the major superpowers of the world not only to recognize Jerusalem as the capital of Israel but to build a building there that signifies Jerusalem as the capital—something that people can go to and see and touch.

On December 6, 2017, President Trump announced that the US Embassy would be moved to Jerusalem to recognize Jews in their homeland, and it was opened there on May 14, 2018—exactly seventy years to the day after the United Nations declared the Jewish people in Israel a nation. When you study prophecy, you'll learn that two of God's favourite numbers are 7 or 70.

If you're looking for something bigger, or a more earth-shattering event, you'll need to read the rest of the book.

TWO
SOMETHING DIFFERENT

IN ORDER TO determine when the Rapture will take place, we need to look at verses that deal with the Rapture and also consider a date, or event, on the calendar. If you can determine the timing of that event, you can think about the Rapture in relation to that timing.

I read through all the verses related to the Rapture, and considered their possible meanings and the context in which they were written. I tried to pick a category (i.e., Pre-Trib, Mid-Trib, Pre-Wrath, or Post-Trib) they would fall into, just to see what I would end up with. Some of them, like Revelation 7:9–14, needed more scriptural context to be placed in the right category. I write about this in Chapter Six.

One passage indicates a month, week, day, and hour for the Rapture, but not a year, because the event spoken of happens every year: *"In a moment, in the twinkling of an eye, at the last trump"* (1 Corinthians 15:52a, KJV). The last trump is the last blowing of a trumpet after it has been played for a good length of time. Every fall in the Hebrew calendar is the Festival of Trumpets.

The Bible contains numerous verses about seasons.[2] I will share two with you.

---

[2] "100 Bible Verses About Seasons," Open Bible, accessed June 6, 2025, https://www.openbible.info/topics/seasons.

WHERE ARE WE?

> For behold, the winter is past; the rain is over and gone. The flowers appear on the earth, the time of singing has come, and the voice of the turtledove is heard in our land. The fig tree ripens its figs, and the vines are in blossom; they give forth fragrance. Arise, my love, my beautiful one, and come away. (Song of Solomon 2:11–13, ESV)

> From the fig tree learn its lesson: as soon as its branch becomes tender and puts out its leaves, you know that summer is near. So also, when you see all these things, you know that he is near, at the very gates. Truly, I say to you, this generation will not pass away until all these things take place. (Matthew 24:32–34, ESV)

I'd like to share thirteen passages of Scripture that support a Pre-Trib Rapture.

> At that time Michael, the great prince who protects your people, will arise. There will be a time of distress such as has not happened from the beginning of nations until then. But at that time your people—everyone whose name is found written in the book—will be delivered. Multitudes who sleep in the dust of the earth will awake: some to everlasting life, others to shame and everlasting contempt. (Daniel 12:1–2)

TWO: SOMETHING DIFFERENT

And I tell you, you are Peter, and on this rock I will build my church, and the gates of hell shall not prevail against it. (Matthew 16:18, ESV)

Two men will be in the field; one will be taken and the other left. Two women will be grinding with a hand mill; one will be taken and the other left. (Matthew 24:40–41)

Be on guard, keep awake. For you do not know when the time will come. It is like a man going on a journey, when he leaves home and puts his servants in charge, each with his work, and commands the doorkeeper to stay awake. Therefore stay awake—for you do not know when the master of the house will come, in the evening, or at midnight, or when the rooster crows, or in the morning—lest he come suddenly and find you asleep. And what I say to you I say to all: Stay awake. (Mark 13:33–37, ESV)

You also must be ready, for the Son of Man is coming at an hour you do not expect (Luke 12:40, ESV)

But stay awake at all times, praying that you may have strength to escape all these things that are going to take place, and to stand before the Son of Man. (Luke 21:36, ESV)

Just as it was in the days of Noah, so will it be in the days of the Son of Man. They were eating and drinking and marrying and being given in marriage, until the day when Noah entered the ark, and the flood came and destroyed them all. Likewise, just as it was in the days of Lot—they were eating and drinking, buying and selling, planting and building, but on the day when Lot went out from Sodom, fire and sulfur rained from heaven and destroyed them all—so will it be on the day when the Son of Man is revealed. (Luke 17:26–30, ESV)

And to wait for his Son from heaven, whom he raised from the dead, Jesus who delivers us from the wrath to come. (1 Thessalonians 1:10, ESV)

Now concerning the times and the seasons, brothers, you have no need to have anything written to you. For you yourselves are fully aware that the day of the Lord will come like a thief in the night. While people are saying, "There is peace and security," then sudden destruction will come upon them as labor pains come upon a pregnant woman, and they will not escape. But you are not in darkness, brothers, for that day to surprise you like a thief. For you are all children of light, children of the day. We are not of the night or of the darkness. So then let us not sleep, as others do, but let us keep awake and be sober. For those who sleep, sleep at night, and those who get drunk, are drunk at night. But since we belong to the day, let us be sober, having put on the breastplate of faith and love, and for a helmet the hope of salvation. For God has

TWO: SOMETHING DIFFERENT

not destined us for wrath, but to obtain salvation through our Lord Jesus Christ, who died for us so that whether we are awake or asleep we might live with him. (1 Thessalonians 5:1–10, ESV)

Remember, then, what you received and heard. Keep it, and repent. If you will not wake up, I will come like a thief, and you will not know at what hour I will come against you. (Revelation 3:3, ESV)

Because you have kept my word about patient endurance, I will keep you from the hour of trial that is coming on the whole world, to try those who dwell on the earth. (Revelation 3:10, ESV)

Calling to the mountains and rocks, "Fall on us and hide us from the face of him who is seated on the throne, and from the wrath of the Lamb." (Revelation 6:16, ESV)

After this I looked, and behold, a great multitude that no one could number, from every nation, from all tribes and peoples and languages, standing before the throne and before the Lamb, clothed in white robes, with palm branches in their hands, and crying out with a loud voice, "Salvation belongs to our God who sits on the throne, and to the Lamb!" And all the angels were standing around the throne and around the elders and the four living creatures, and they fell on their faces before the throne and worshiped God, saying, "Amen!

WHERE ARE WE?

> Blessing and glory and wisdom and thanksgiving and honor and power and might be to our God forever and ever! Amen." Then one of the elders addressed me, saying, "Who are these, clothed in white robes, and from where have they come?" I said to him, "Sir, you know." And he said to me, "These are the ones coming out of the great tribulation. They have washed their robes and made them white in the blood of the Lamb." (Revelation 7:9–14, ESV)

To read more on this topic, I recommend an article by Daymond Duck.[3]

I'd like to share twelve passages that support a Mid-Trib, Pre-Wrath Rapture.

> He will speak against the Most High and oppress his holy people and try to change the set times and the laws. The holy people will be delivered into his hands for a time, times and half a time. (Daniel 7:25)

> "At that time shall arise Michael, the great prince who has charge of your people. And there shall be a time of trouble, such as never has been since there was a nation till that time. But at that time your people shall be delivered, everyone whose name shall be found written in the book. And many of those who sleep in the dust of the earth shall awake, some to everlasting life, and some to shame and

---

[3] Daymond Duck, "36 Pre-Trib Rapture Texts," Rapture Ready, October 26, 2010, https://www.raptureready.com/2010/10/26/36-pre-trib-rapture-texts/.

TWO: SOMETHING DIFFERENT

everlasting contempt. And those who are wise shall shine like the brightness of the sky above; and those who turn many to righteousness, like the stars forever and ever. But you, Daniel, shut up the words and seal the book, until the time of the end. Many shall run to and fro, and knowledge shall increase." Then I, Daniel, looked, and behold, two others stood, one on this bank of the stream and one on that bank of the stream. And someone said to the man clothed in linen, who was above the waters of the stream, "How long shall it be till the end of these wonders?" And I heard the man clothed in linen, who was above the waters of the stream; he raised his right hand and his left hand toward heaven and swore by him who lives forever that it would be for a time, times, and half a time, and that when the shattering of the power of the holy people comes to an end all these things would be finished. (Daniel 12:1–7, ESV)

And from the time that the regular burnt offering is taken away and the abomination that makes desolate is set up, there shall be 1,290 days. (Daniel 12:11, ESV)

As he sat on the Mount of Olives, the disciples came to him privately, saying, "Tell us, when will these things be, and what will be the sign of your coming and of the end of the age?" (Matthew 24:3, ESV)

Then will appear the sign of the Son of Man in heaven. And then all the peoples of the earth will mourn when they see the Son of Man coming on the clouds of heaven, with power and great glory. And he will send his angels with a loud trumpet call, and they will gather his elect from the four winds, from one end of the heavens to the other. (Matthew 24:30–31)

Truly, I say to you, this generation will not pass away until all these things take place. (Matthew 24:34, ESV)

But when you see the abomination of desolation standing where he ought not to be (let the reader understand), then let those who are in Judea flee to the mountains … And they will see the Son of Man coming in clouds with great power and glory. And then he will send out the angels and gather his elect from the four winds, from the ends of the earth to the ends of heaven. (Mark 13:14, 26–27, ESV)

For the Lord himself will descend from heaven with a cry of command, with the voice of an archangel, and with the sound of the trumpet of God. And the dead in Christ will rise first. Then we who are alive, who are left, will be caught up together with them in the clouds to meet the Lord in the air, and so we will always be with the Lord. (1 Thessalonians 4:16–17, ESV)

Therefore we ourselves boast about you in the churches of God for your steadfastness and faith in all your

TWO: SOMETHING DIFFERENT

persecutions and in the afflictions that you are enduring. (2 Thessalonians 1:4, ESV)

I know your works, your toil and your patient endurance, and how you cannot bear with those who are evil, but have tested those who call themselves apostles and are not, and found them to be false. (Revelation 2:2, ESV)

After this I looked, and behold, a great multitude that no one could number, from every nation, from all tribes and peoples and languages, standing before the throne and before the Lamb, clothed in white robes, with palm branches in their hands. (Revelation 7:9, ESV)

Then I saw thrones, and seated on them were those to whom the authority to judge was committed. Also I saw the souls of those who had been beheaded for the testimony of Jesus and for the word of God, and those who had not worshiped the beast or its image and had not received its mark on their foreheads or their hands. They came to life and reigned with Christ for a thousand years. (Revelation 20:4, ESV)

To learn more about this perspective, I encourage you to read Patrick Oh's thoughts.[4]

---

[4] Patrick Oh, "Exploring the Mid-Tribulation Rapture View: A Biblical Perspective," Medium, September 23, 2023, https://medium.com/@patrick-oh-sglion65/exploring-the-mid-tribulation-rapture-view-a-biblical-perspective-93a5586b8d2c.

WHERE ARE WE?

I'd like to share two passages that support the Post-Trib view of the Rapture.

> Jesus told them another parable: "The kingdom of heaven is like a man who sowed good seed in his field. But while everyone was sleeping, his enemy came and sowed weeds among the wheat, and went away. When the wheat sprouted and formed ears, then the weeds also appeared. The owner's servants came to him and said, 'Sir, didn't you sow good seed in your field? Where then did the weeds come from?' 'An enemy did this,' he replied. The servants asked him, 'Do you want us to go and pull them up?' 'No,' he answered, 'because while you are pulling up the weeds, you may uproot the wheat with them. Let both grow together until the harvest. At that time I will tell the harvesters: first collect the weeds and tie them in bundles to be burned; then gather the wheat and bring it into my barn.'" He told them another parable: "The kingdom of heaven is like a mustard seed, which a man took and planted in his field. Though it is the smallest of all seeds, yet when it grows, it is the largest of garden plants and becomes a tree, so that the birds come and perch in its branches." He told them still another parable: "The kingdom of heaven is like yeast that a woman took and mixed into about thirty kilograms of flour until it worked all through the dough." Jesus spoke all these things to the crowd in parables; he did not say anything to them without using a parable. So was fulfilled what

TWO: SOMETHING DIFFERENT

was spoken through the prophet: "I will open my mouth in parables, I will utter things hidden since the creation of the world." Then he left the crowd and went into the house. His disciples came to him and said, "Explain to us the parable of the weeds in the field." He answered, "The one who sowed the good seed is the Son of Man. The field is the world, and the good seed stands for the people of the kingdom. The weeds are the people of the evil one, and the enemy who sows them is the devil. The harvest is the end of the age, and the harvesters are angels. As the weeds are pulled up and burned in the fire, so it will be at the end of the age. The Son of Man will send out his angels, and they will weed out of his kingdom everything that causes sin and all who do evil. They will throw them into the blazing furnace, where there will be weeping and gnashing of teeth. Then the righteous will shine like the sun in the kingdom of their Father. Whoever has ears, let them hear." (Matthew 13:24–43)

Whoever has ears, let them hear. "If anyone is to go into captivity, into captivity they will go. If anyone is to be killed with the sword, with the sword they will be killed." This calls for patient endurance and faithfulness on the part of God's people. (Revelation 13:9–10)

If you're looking for a Rapture date that translates directly to a modern-day calendar, I can't find one. Every reference to a period of time in connection to the Rapture is connected to the Tribulation.

THREE
IS THERE A RAPTURE?

SOME PEOPLE WITH less knowledge of Bible prophecy claim that the word "rapture" isn't in the Bible. A good reply to this is that the word "Bible" isn't in the Bible either, nor are the words "trinity" or "Christianity." So if you don't believe in something because the word describing it isn't in the Bible, then do you not believe in the Bible, the Trinity, or Christianity? In that case, what do you believe in?

A husband and wife are empty-nesters. The husband leaves the house, and two minutes later he gets a phone call from his wife, asking him where her phone is. He asks if she's still at home, and she says yes. He asks if anyone else is there, and she says no. He asks what's in her hands. She wedges her phone between her shoulder and her ear, looks at her hands, and says, "My hands are empty. Enough with the questions—where is my phone?"

Her husband replies, "So when you phoned me to tell me you'd lost your phone, whose phone did you use to call me?" The moral of the story is that just because you can't see something doesn't mean it isn't there.

One must remember that most modern-day versions of the Bible come from manuscripts that were discovered after the printing of the King James Version, which are translations from Hebrew and Aramaic and Greek.

WHERE ARE WE?

The New International Version of 1 Thessalonians 4:16–17 reads as follows:

> For the Lord himself will come down from heaven, with a loud command, with the voice of the archangel and with the trumpet call of God, and the dead in Christ will rise first. 17 After that, we who are still alive and are left will be caught up together with them in the clouds to meet the Lord in the air. And so we will be with the Lord forever.

The King James Version of the same passage reads:

> For the Lord himself shall descend from heaven with a shout, with the voice of the archangel, and with the trump of God: and the dead in Christ shall rise first: Then we which are alive and remain shall be caught up together with them in the clouds, to meet the Lord in the air: and so shall we ever be with the Lord.

In the Greek version of this passage, you'll find the word *harpagēsometha*, which means "we shall be caught up" or "taken away." The translators working on the King James Version chose to include the meaning of the word "rapture" instead of the word itself. The English word "rapture" is derived from the Latin verb *rapio*, which was used in the Latin Vulgate to translate *harpazō*. *Rapio* is used in verse 17, when Paul says "will be *caught up*," and it's from this association that we get the word "rapture." Long before this word was ubiquitous in modern culture, however, the early Church

THREE: IS THERE A RAPTURE?

Fathers wrestled with the concept of the rapture (even if they didn't necessarily call it by that word) by examining the above-mentioned verse and other Scriptures relating to the end times.

> Listen, I tell you a mystery: We will not all sleep, but we will all be changed—in a flash, in the twinkling of an eye, at the last trumpet. For the trumpet will sound, the dead will be raised imperishable, and we will be changed. For the perishable must clothe itself with the imperishable, and the mortal with immortality. When the perishable has been clothed with the imperishable, and the mortal with immortality, then the saying that is written will come true: "Death has been swallowed up in victory." (1 Corinthians 15:51–54)

> But stay awake at all times, praying that you may have strength to escape all these things that are going to take place, and to stand before the Son of Man. (Luke 21:36, ESV)

> Brothers and sisters, we do not want you to be uninformed about those who sleep in death, so that you do not grieve like the rest of mankind, who have no hope. For we believe that Jesus died and rose again, and so we believe that God will bring with Jesus those who have fallen asleep in him. According to the Lord's word, we tell you that we who are still alive, who are left until the coming of the Lord, will certainly not precede those who have fallen

asleep. For the Lord himself will come down from heaven, with a loud command, with the voice of the archangel and with the trumpet call of God, and the dead in Christ will rise first. After that, we who are still alive and are left will be caught up together with them in the clouds to meet the Lord in the air. And so we will be with the Lord forever. (1 Thessalonians 4:13–17)

Since you have kept my command to endure patiently, I will also keep you from the hour of trial that is going to come on the whole world to test the inhabitants of the earth. (Revelation 3:10)

There is strong evidence for a Rapture, which is why I'm writing this book. Whether you choose to research when you think it will happen is not the most important thing in life. The most important thing in life on this planet is that when the day of the Rapture does come, you won't be left behind but will have your ticket to heaven.

FOUR
DIFFERENT ANSWERS

I'M THINKING THERE should be numerous ways to answer the question of when the Rapture will occur.

1. At this moment in time, it's not possible to give the day or the hour.
2. The Bible says He will come at a time we don't expect.
3. It depends on whether the Rapture takes place before the Tribulation or mid-way through it. There are some die-hard proponents for both.
4. Not today, as some pre-requisite prophecies haven't been fulfilled.
5. Some people are happy and content with not knowing the day or the hour, and I don't want to say anything to disturb them.
6. Forty years ago, people were saying we were living in the end times, and today they're saying that we're living in the end days of the end times.
7. It's a very simple question with a long, complex response that simply leads to a segment of time.
8. The Bible contains many references to the Rapture in relation to the Tribulation. If one could figure out when the Tribulation would take place, then they'd have a better idea of when the Rapture would occur.

9. I could talk for three hours. How much time do I have?
10. How much do you want to know?
11. How scared do you want to be?
12. If there were ten people in Canada to whom you'd pose that question, I might be one of them. I've spent thirteen years researching the topic—probably approaching three thousand hours.
13. A popular internet catchphrase a couple of years ago was "Anytime between two minutes from now to two hundred years from now."
14. There are some very strong opinions out there, but most verses support two options: a Pre-Trib Rapture and a Mid-Trib Rapture. This gives you a time variable of four years. Even if you know when the Tribulation will take place, that still leaves you with a four-year time slot. The most important thing is to believe in the Lord with all your heart so that when that day happens, you're not left behind.
15. If you're focusing on the fact that no one knows the day or the hour, say it over a few times. Does it say anything about the week, month, or year?
16. In Matthew 24:36, Jesus says that no one knows the day or the hour. Matthew was written in AD 85, Mark in AD 90, Luke in AD 80–90, and John in AD 90–100. These four gospels are memoirs of the past, written about the days when Jesus walked on the earth. In AD 96, the book of Revelation was written, about sixty years after Christ was on earth. Revelation 1:1 reads, *"The revelation of Jesus Christ, which God gave him to show to his servants the things that*

FOUR: DIFFERENT ANSWERS

must soon take place. He made it known by sending his angel to his servant John." God gave Jesus information, and He gave it to an angel, who gave it to John, who gave it to us. To look at this another way, anything that was a secret before AD 96 might now be revealed, including the meaning of Matthew 24:36.

This leads us to Revelation 3:3. This verse can be hard to read or understand, as it contains a double negative. "Remember therefore how thou hast received and heard, and hold fast, and repent, if therefore thou shalt not watch, I will come as a thief, and thou shalt not know what hour I will come upon thee" (KJV) The same verse in the ESV reads as follows: *"Remember, then, what you received and heard. Keep it, and repent. If you will not wake up, I will come like a thief, and you will not know at what hour I will come against you."* What if you're awake? Does this mean that the day and the hour are still a secret for only God to know? If you look at all the evidence, you'll see that some angels in heaven would have to have known for the last two thousand years. Does this mean that it's possible for us to know the hour? At this point in time, with 100 per cent certainty, I would say no. If the Tribulation had already started, and it started on an approximate date of January 12 and we were still here, and you're looking for 99 per cent certainty, the answer would be yes.

17. A popular phrase from 1970 to 2010 was to say that we were "living in the end times." The people who were saying

that, though, no longer say it. The new catchphrase today is that we're living in the "end days of the end times."

18. If you were to ask when the Rapture will occur, and someone quoted Matthew 24:36, about no one knowing the day or the hour, you could respond with:
    a) That's a verse in the Bible, which is good.
    b) That verse relates to the subject, which is great.
    c) That's the first in a series of important verses on end-times prophecy. Without knowing the series, it's extremely difficult to understand end-times prophecy.
    d) It's awesome that you know that verse.

In a recent survey, 47 per cent of Christians and 39 per cent of the general public in the US claim to believe that we are living in the end times. Even atheists, at 9 per cent, believe that we're in the end times.[5] If we're getting that close, I think I should look into it. Approximately thirteen years ago, I started researching at a rate of 150 hours per year. I've looked at a lot of material. That may sound impressive, but it's not nearly as impressive as the amount of information the Lord has allowed me to find. If you find this interesting and would like more information, there is material out there.

---

[5] Jeff Diamant, "About Four-in-Ten U.S. Adults Believe Humanity Is 'Living in the End Times,'" Pew Research Center, December 8, 2022, https://www.pewresearch.org/short-reads/2022/12/08/about-four-in-ten-u-s-adults-believe-humanity-is-living-in-the-end-times/.

FIVE
THE SERIES—IS IT POSSIBLE TO KNOW WHEN THE RAPTURE WILL OCCUR?

IN ORDER TO know if it's possible to know when the Rapture will occur, we need to understand the series. If we have no knowledge of the series, we'll never understand biblical end-time prophecy. What is the series? We need to go back to about three thousand years before Christ was born. Back then, if you sinned and wanted forgiveness, you had to shed the blood of a sacrificial animal. When Christ came and His blood was shed on the cross, something changed. We no longer needed to sacrifice animals to gain forgiveness. We only needed to ask for forgiveness, and it was granted.

Matthew 24:36 is an often quoted verse, and it was possibly written between AD 80 to 90: *"But about that day or hour no one knows, not even the angels in heaven, nor the Son, but only the Father."* Jesus said this while on earth, sometime between AD 25 and 35.

The second verse we'll look at is from Revelation, which was written in around AD 95. It wasn't written as memoirs of the past but for the present and the future: *"The revelation of Jesus Christ which God gave him to show to his servants the things that must soon take place. He made it known by sending his angel to his servant John"* (Revelation 1:1, ESV). So sixty years after Jesus was on earth, God gave Him information, which He gave it to an angel, who gave it to John. In it, God released some secrets.

WHERE ARE WE?

This leads us to a third verse: *"If therefore thou shalt not watch, I will come on thee as a thief, and thou shalt not know what hour I will come upon thee"* (Revelation 3:3, KJV). So if you're observant, researching, awake, and watching, this verse says it's possible to know the hour. So does Matthew 24:36 still hold true today, or has there been a change?

For some people, asking if we can know the time of the Rapture is a bold question, but we need dig deeper into Scripture. Let's start with John 14:2–3.

> My Father's house has many rooms; if that were not so, would I have told you that I am going there to prepare a place for you? And if I go and prepare a place for you, I will come back and take you to be with me that you also may be where I am.

Jesus has gone to prepare heaven for us. We should do some math just to get an idea of what's involved in that. We could compare it to building a house on earth. Generally in construction, if someone wants something built, they need to answer three basic questions: How big is it? When do you want to start? When is the move-in date?

Let's say three people can build a twelve-room house in four months. That works out to one person building one room a month. In Jesus's time, there had been approximately 40 billion people who had ever lived into adulthood. If the Rapture took place one hundred years after Jesus ascended to heaven, He would need to build 40 billion x 30 per cent, or 12 billion rooms in one hundred years. That's 120,000,000 in one year, or 57,692 rooms per hour.

If the Rapture took place two thousand years later, that would mean 24 billion people heading to heaven in the last six thousand years. Let's say Jesus were to build 24 billion rooms in two thousand years. That works out to 5,770 rooms per hour.

Side note: The size of our new heaven is massive, at 1,400 miles high, 1,400 miles wide, and 1,400 miles high. This gives you 2,744,000,000 cubic miles. *"I did not see a temple in the city, because the Lord God Almighty and the Lamb are its temple"* (Revelation 21:22). This would calculate out to twelve people for every cubic mile, brings you to 613,324,800 sq ft. That's not really just a big room that's a massive building with hundreds of rooms. Going to need a motorcycle just to get to the other side of your house.

Clearly, in order to get it done, Jesus would need to know how big it's to be, when He needs to start, and the move-in date?

Revelation chapters 21 and 22 outline the details of heaven, and they were written around AD 94—at least sixty years after Jesus returned to heaven. In order to complete the task, He'd need to know the answers to all three questions very shortly after His ascension. I would expect He had access to the information in less than a year.

In Matthew 4:4, Jesus says, *"It is written, 'Man shall not live by bread alone, but on every word that comes from the mouth of God.'"* This shows us that we're not supposed to live our lives based on one verse, such as *"nobody knows the day or hour."* In the latter days, we'll be able to piece some information together, as *"knowledge shall be increased"* (Daniel 12:4, KJV). Jesus spoke

WHERE ARE WE?

the words in Matthew 24:36 while on earth, which leads us to John 14:28: *"You heard me say, 'I am going away and I am coming back to you.' If you loved me, you would be glad that I am going to the Father, for the Father is greater than I."* In John 20:17, Jesus says, *"Do not cling to me, for I have not yet ascended to the Father; but go to my brothers and say to them, 'I am ascending to my Father and your Father, to my God and your God'"* (ESV).

Notice that it doesn't say whether Jesus is going to talk to God, or God is going to talk to Jesus. To possibly understand this further, we need to look at Moses in Numbers 20:8–12.

> Take the staff, and you and your brother Aaron gather the assembly together. Speak to that rock before their eyes and it will pour out its water. You will bring water out of the rock for the community so they and their livestock can drink." So Moses took the staff from the Lord's presence, just as he commanded him. He and Aaron gathered the assembly together in front of the rock and Moses said to them, "Listen, you rebels, must we bring you water out of this rock?" Then Moses raised his arm and struck the rock twice with his staff. Water gushed out, and the community and their livestock drank. But the Lord said to Moses and Aaron, "Because you did not trust in me enough to honor me as holy in the sight of the Israelites, you will not bring this community into the land I give them."

Moses was punished for not following God's instructions perfectly. Let's compare that to Jesus in John 2.

FIVE: THE SERIES—IS IT POSSIBLE TO KNOW WHEN THE...

On the third day a wedding took place at Cana in Galilee. Jesus' mother was there, and Jesus and his disciples had also been invited to the wedding. When the wine was gone, Jesus' mother said to him, "They have no more wine." "Woman, why do you involve me?" Jesus replied. "My hour has not yet come." His mother said to the servants, "Do whatever he tells you." Nearby stood six stone water jars, the kind used by the Jews for ceremonial washing, each holding from twenty to thirty gallons. Jesus said to the servants, "Fill the jars with water"; so they filled them to the brim. Then he told them, "Now draw some out and take it to the master of the banquet." They did so, and the master of the banquet tasted the water that had been turned into wine. He did not realize where it had come from, though the servants who had drawn the water knew. Then he called the bridegroom aside and said, "Everyone brings out the choice wine first and then the cheaper wine after the guests have had too much to drink; but you have saved the best till now." What Jesus did here in Cana of Galilee was the first of the signs through which he revealed his glory; and his disciples believed in him. (John 2:1–11).

In verse 4, we learn that Jesus performed a miracle before His time.

"Abraham is our father," they answered. "If you were Abraham's children," said Jesus, "then you would do what

WHERE ARE WE?

> Abraham did. As it is, you are looking for a way to kill me, a man who has told you the truth that I heard from God. Abraham did not do such things. You are doing the works of your own father." "We are not illegitimate children," they protested. "The only Father we have is God himself." (John 8:39–41)

In verse 40, Jesus says He is a man, not God.

> And He went a little beyond them, and fell on His face and prayed, saying, "My Father, if it is possible, let this cup pass from Me; yet not as I will, but as You will." And He came to the disciples and found them sleeping, and He said to Peter, "So, you men could not keep watch with Me for one hour? Keep watching and praying, so that you do not come into temptation; the spirit is [p]willing, but the flesh is weak." He went away again a second time and prayed, saying, "My Father, if this cup cannot pass away unless I drink from it, Your will be done." (Matthew 26:39–42)

Here we see Jesus twice asking to do something different.

Jesus said He was a man and was making decisions, but He didn't know if they were perfect or not. It's possible that Jesus didn't know how God would react to the decisions He made while on earth, or if one imperfect decision would result in punishment or consequences, such as keeping the Rapture date a secret a lot longer than when Jesus got to heaven, perhaps even two thousand years. If a person can grasp this, then they should be able to

FIVE: THE SERIES—IS IT POSSIBLE TO KNOW WHEN THE...

grasp the short version, which is that while He was on earth, Jesus didn't know when the Rapture and Tribulation would happen, and He didn't know if or when He would ever be told.

"Remember, then, what you received and heard. Keep it, and repent. If you will not wake up, I will come like a thief, and you will not know at what hour I will come against you" (Revelation 3:3, ESV). What does it mean to watch or "wake up"? This could be interpreted as people who are doing research and paying attention to where we are. This could eliminate 99 per cent of all humans. The phrase "not wake up" can also indicate that someone is asleep. What does "asleep" mean?

- We read about Lazarus in John 11. Lazarus was sick and then died, but Jesus said he was sleeping.
- In God's mind, the dead shall rise first in the Rapture, so were they dead or just sleeping?
- Every night, humans need sleep so that we can be awake during the day.
- We can be awake but zoned out or so mentally distracted that we're not paying attention to what's happening around us.

From this we can assume that if we don't "watch," as in pay attention to current events, or if we don't research the timing of the Rapture, we won't know the hour.

Revelation 3:3 seems to reference two different kinds of people: those who watch and those who don't. So why is this verse in the Bible? Because God wanted us to know that one group of people wouldn't know the hour. So what if we do watch? In my mind, a person can't argue with the wording, and we're left with the following thought. At some point in time, those who watch will know the hour. We're not supposed to base our faith on just one verse, so here are some other passages to support this argument.

> Now, brothers and sisters, about times and dates we do not need to write to you, for you know very well that the day of the Lord will come like a thief in the night. While people are saying, "Peace and safety," destruction will come on them suddenly, as labor pains on a pregnant woman, and they will not escape. But you, brothers and sisters, are not in darkness so that this day should surprise you like a thief. You are all children of the light and children of the day. We do not belong to the night or to the darkness. (1 Thessalonians 5:1–5)

First Thessalonians was written around AD 50–52 by Paul.

"Besides this you know the time, that the hour has come for you to wake from sleep. For salvation is nearer to us now than when we first believed" (Romans 13:11, ESV). Romans was written around AD 57 by Paul.

"The end of all things is near. Therefore be alert and of sober mind so that you may pray" (1 Peter 4:7). First Peter was written between AD 62 and 64.

"Wherefore he saith, Awake thou that sleepest, and arise from the dead, and Christ shall give thee light" (Ephesians 5:14, KJV). Ephesians was written between AD 60 and 62 by Paul.

FIVE: THE SERIES—IS IT POSSIBLE TO KNOW WHEN THE...

"If he comes suddenly, do not let him find you sleeping. What I say to you, I say to everyone: 'Watch!'" (Mark 13:36–37).

Be dressed ready for service and keep your lamps burning, like servants waiting for their master to return from a wedding banquet, so that when he comes and knocks they can immediately open the door for him. It will be good for those servants whose master finds them watching when he comes. Truly I tell you, he will dress himself to serve, will have them recline at the table and will come and wait on them. It will be good for those servants whose master finds them ready, even if he comes in the middle of the night or toward daybreak. But understand this: If the owner of the house had known at what hour the thief was coming, he would not have let his house be broken into. You also must be ready, because the Son of Man will come at an hour when you do not expect him." (Luke 12:35–40)

Just as it was in the days of Noah, so will it be in the days of the Son of Man. They were eating and drinking and marrying and being given in marriage, until the day when Noah entered the ark, and the flood came and destroyed them all. Likewise, just as it was in the days of Lot—they were eating and drinking, buying and selling, planting and building, but on the day when Lot went out from Sodom, fire and sulfur rained from heaven and destroyed them all— so will it be on the day when the Son of Man is revealed. (Luke 17:26–30, ESV)

WHERE ARE WE?

"And they were unaware until the flood came and swept them all away, so will be the coming of the Son of Man" (Matthew 24:39, ESV).

We also must keep in mind 2 Timothy 3:16–17: *"All Scripture is breathed out by God and profitable for teaching, for reproof, for correction, and for training in righteousness, that the man of God may be complete, equipped for every good work"* (ESV).

As all scripture is God-breathed, we need to consider that at some point in time, there will be some people on earth who will know the hour. I don't believe that the time has come yet. There's not enough information out there to narrow it down to the hour. But maybe knowing the hour will be a clue to finding the week, the month, and the year.

SIX
WHEN WILL THE RAPTURE TAKE PLACE?

THERE ARE FOUR basic beliefs surrounding the timing of the Rapture, and they are Pre-Trib, Mid-Trib, Pre-Wrath, and Post-Trib.

Robert Breaker presents a theory that God's bride is the Church.[6] It doesn't make sense that God's bride will be given over to Satan for part of the Tribulation; therefore, God will take His bride before the Tribulation. Nice thoughts, but does the Bible support this concept?

> After this I looked, and there before me was a great multitude that no one could count, from every nation, tribe, people and language, standing before the throne and before the Lamb. They were wearing white robes and were holding palm branches in their hands. And they cried out in a loud voice: "Salvation belongs to our God, who sits on the throne, and to the Lamb." All the angels were standing around the throne and around the elders and the four living creatures. They fell down on their faces before the throne and worshiped God, saying: "Amen! Praise and glory and wisdom and thanks and honor and power and strength be to our God for ever and ever. Amen!" Then one of the elders asked me, "These in white robes—who are they, and where

---

[6] Robert Breaker, "When Exactly Is the Mark of the Beast?" YouTube Video, October 25, 2021, 7:30–14:30, https://www.youtube.com/watch?v=JesYp-hiLM0

did they come from?" I answered, "Sir, you know." And he said, "These are they who have come out of the great tribulation; they have washed their robes and made them white in the blood of the Lamb." (Revelation 7:9–14)

These verses imply that the people standing there were not in the rapture, as they were not part of the long-awaited group. This can be used to support the Pre-Trib position.

If you consider Daniel's seventy weeks, we (the Church) were not in the first sixty-nine weeks. So why would we be in the seventieth week?[7]

"Be always on the watch, and pray that you may be able to escape all that is about to happen, and that you may be able to stand before the Son of Man" (Luke 21:36)

And Jesus came and said to them, "All authority in heaven and on earth has been given to me. Go therefore and make disciples of all nations, baptizing them in the name of the Father and of the Son and of the Holy Spirit, teaching them to observe all that I have commanded you. And behold, I am with you always, to the end of the age." (Matthew 28:18–20, ESV)

Calling to the mountains and rocks, "Fall on us and hide us from the face of him who is seated on the throne, and from

---

[7] BR Ministries, "Prophecy Update—February 2022—The Rapture—Brett Meador," YouTube video, February 6, 2022, 1:29:48 (begin at 1:22:00 mark), https://www.youtube.com/watch?v=X_PBlGjJ8Ok.

SIX: WHEN WILL THE RAPTURE TAKE PLACE?

the wrath of the Lamb, for the great day of their wrath has come, and who can stand?" (Revelation 6:16–17, ESV)

For God has not destined us for wrath, but to obtain salvation through our Lord Jesus Christ, who died for us so that whether we are awake or asleep we might live with him. Therefore encourage one another and build one another up, just as you are doing. (1 Thessalonians 5:9–11, ESV)

"… and to wait for his Son from heaven, whom he raised from the dead, Jesus who delivers us from the wrath to come" (1 Thessalonians 1:10, ESV).

The tribulation is supposed to start with the announcement of a seven-year peace plan by the Antichrist. This announcement will also reveal the identity of the Antichrist.

He will confirm a covenant with many for one 'seven.' In the middle of the 'seven' he will put an end to sacrifice and offering …" (Daniel 9:27)

Concerning the coming of our Lord Jesus Christ and our being gathered to him, we ask you, brothers and sisters, not to become easily unsettled or alarmed by the teaching allegedly from us—whether by a prophecy or by word of mouth or by letter—asserting that the day of the Lord has already come. Don't let anyone deceive you in any way, for that day will not come until the rebellion occurs and the man of lawlessness is revealed, the man doomed to destruction. He will oppose and will exalt himself over everything that is called God or is worshiped, so that he sets himself up in God's temple, proclaiming himself to be God. (2 Thessalonians 2:1–4)

The Pre-Trib position is not compatible with the passage above.

In Daniel 12 there comes a time of distress.

At that time Michael, the great prince who protects your people, will arise. There will be a time of distress such as has not happened from the beginning of nations until then. But at that time your people—everyone whose name is found written in the book—will be delivered. Multitudes who sleep in the dust of the earth will awake: some to everlasting life, others to shame and everlasting contempt. Those who are wise will shine like the brightness of the heavens, and those who lead many to righteousness, like the stars for ever and ever. (Daniel 12:1–3)

This passage refers to the Rapture after a time of distress; therefore, we could conclude that the Rapture occurs after the Tribulation starts.

"But you, Daniel, roll up and seal the words of the scroll until the time of the end. Many will go here and there to increase knowledge." Then I, Daniel, looked, and there before me stood two others, one on this bank of the river and one on the opposite bank. One of them said to the

SIX: WHEN WILL THE RAPTURE TAKE PLACE?

man clothed in linen, who was above the waters of the river, "How long will it be before these astonishing things are fulfilled?" The man clothed in linen, who was above the waters of the river, lifted his right hand and his left hand toward heaven, and I heard him swear by him who lives forever, saying, "It will be for a time, times and half a time. When the power of the holy people has been finally broken, all these things will be completed." (Daniel 12:4–7)

A "time" can be interpreted as one year. Times can be interpreted as two years. Half a time would be half a year. This gives us three and a half years.

In verse 7, when it speaks of the power of the Holy Spirit being broken, does this mean the Holy Spirit will be here on earth in the first three and a half years of the Tribulation but not the last half? Let's consider different translations of Revelation 3:10.

Because thou hast kept the word of my patience, I also will keep thee from the hour of temptation, which shall come upon all the world, to try them that dwell upon the earth. (KJV)

Because you have kept my word about patient endurance, I will keep you from the hour of trial that is coming on the whole world, to try those who dwell on the earth. (ESV)

Since you have kept my command to endure patiently, I will also keep you from the hour of trial that is going to come on the whole world to test the inhabitants of the earth. (NIV)

From this verse, we can gather two things: He will rescue the Christians before things get really bad, which reaffirms the Rapture, and a trial will come on the whole world to test the inhabitants of the earth. And we will not be here. So Revelation 3:10 is not compatible with a Post-Trib position.

Daniel chapters 10 to 12 provide background to the timing of the Tribulation and Rapture. Daniel 12:11 reads, *"From the time that the daily sacrifice is abolished and the abomination that causes desolation is set up, there will be 1,290 days."* That's three and a half years plus twelve days. Daniel 12:12 reads, *"Blessed is the one who waits for and reaches the end of the 1,335 days."*

Another passage to consider comes from Matthew: *"Nation will rise against nation, and kingdom against kingdom. There will be famines and earthquakes in various places. 8 All these are the beginning of birth pains"* (Matthew 24:7–8).

Daniel 12:11 and Matthew 24:15 provide the same time period, which is 1,290 days. Daniel 12:12 cites 1,335 days, and Matthew 24:30 seems to reinforce that.

Does this mean the rapture will take place 1,335 days after the Tribulation starts, or three and a half years and two months? If the 666 implant/tattoo element is enforced at three and a half years, how long can people survive without buying food? Most people keep a week or less worth of food in the house. If you know something bad is coming, you can try to stock up. But for how long can you store food if you don't have the space or equipment? Will you

SIX: WHEN WILL THE RAPTURE TAKE PLACE?

even have electricity? It might be there, but will you be able to buy food or pay the utility bills without the implant? You will likely need enough food to last for two months. I suspect that most people don't realize how bad it could get.

Another passage to consider is 1 Corinthians 15:52: *"in a flash, in the twinkling of an eye, at the last trumpet. For the trumpet will sound, the dead will be raised imperishable, and we will be changed."* Is Paul referring to God's seven trumpets in the book of Revelation? If so, then combined with Daniel 10:11, we would know the day. But how would we know the hour? We need a view that's compatible with Revelation 3:3.

"But stay awake at all times, praying that you may have strength to escape all these things that are going to take place, and to stand before the Son of Man" (Luke 21:36, ESV). And just when you have something figured out, you read Luke 12:40: *"You also must be ready, because the Son of Man will come at an hour when you do not expect him."*

Is it possible there are two Raptures? One just before the Tribulation and the second at the 1,335-day mark after the Tribulation starts? This would explain why there are passages supporting a Pre-Trib Rapture and passages supporting a 1,335-day Rapture.[8]

---

[8] Get Ready Jesus Is Coming, "7 Reasons Why the Tribulation Begins This Year! New Revelations! Rapture!" YouTube video, April 24, 2022, 29:17, https://www.youtube.com/watch?app=desktop&v=VXsvK4E8wxc.

SEVEN
DOUBLE MEANING

"From the time that the daily sacrifice is abolished and the abomination that causes desolation is set up, there will be 1,290 days. Blessed is the one who waits for and reaches the end of the 1,335 days" (Daniel 12:11–12).

IN 692, THE Dome of the Rock was built, which cut off access to what the Jewish people considered the official site for sacrifices. What if the days have a double meaning and were actually years? What would the numbers look like if you added 692 and 1,290? It works out to 1982. What happened in 1982? Year of peace for the Lebanon war, which started and ended in 1982.

What happens if you add 692 and 1,335? It comes to the year 2027. This could be interpreted as just a weird coincidence, but God doesn't do coincidences.

Robert Breaker discusses this in a YouTube video,[9] and at the 26:40, mark, he refers to "peace and security," in reference to Revelation 13:2:

> And the beast which I saw was like unto a leopard, and his feet were as the feet of a bear, and his mouth as the mouth

---

[9] Robert Breaker, "Could the Rapture Come in 2022," YouTube video, December 31, 2021, 40:45, https://www.youtube.com/watch?v=RBTDVUWMXDs&t=950s.

of a lion: and the dragon gave him his power, and his seat, and great authority. (KJV)

In 1 Corinthians 15:52, Paul refers to the "last trump." So what is the last trump? Is this a connection to Trump being president? Some people believe so. Jewish tradition says that the last trump is the blowing of the last trumpet at the end of the festival of trumpets. Does the Hebrew calendar have a festival of trumpets? Yes. So when is the Hebrew festival of trumpets? Every year on September 7–8.

If this all works out, then that would explain a connection with Revelation 3:3, which implies that at some point in time, those who watch will know the hour—in other words, the day the Tribulation starts will reveal the month, week, day, and hour of the Rapture.

Counting backwards 1,335 days from September 8 brings us to January 12 as an approximate start day, depending on the leap years, for this to work out.

I used the website http://www.easysurf.cc/ndate1.htm to calculate the days.

EIGHT
TRACKING

DURING THE TRIBULATION, there will be personal identification numbering and tracking. So how close are we now?

I came across a news item on the internet about a person requesting information in her file, specifically her Alexa. They sent her 3,532 audio recordings of people talking in her house.[10]

My phone was recently stolen. I got a new phone, and in only a few minutes, I had everything on my new phone that had been on my old phone. One of the apps I use is called "Keep Notes," which I use as a shopping list as well as different categories of projects I should work on. When I finish a project, the item goes to a ticked file. All nine categories of files and all ticked items were there.

Have you ever noticed that if you Google an item, the next time you're on your phone or computer, you get ads about that item? Somewhere there's a computer that logs what I'm buying and what I'm working on. It just generally copies everything that's on my phone. For the tracking part of the Tribulation, the technology is not only already here, but is already being used.

---

[10] Adam Smith, "Woman Finds Vast Trove of Voice Recordings Collected by Amazon's Alexa—And You Can Hear Yours," Independent, October 23, 2021, www.independent.co.uk/life-style/gadgets-and-tech/alexa-amazon-echo-voice-recordings-b1943527.html.

NINE
DANIEL'S SEVENTY WEEKS

THIS PROPHECY CONTAINS a couple of important points. In the seventy weeks that are decreed, Jerusalem is to be rebuilt and then destroyed. The Messiah will appear at the end of sixty-nine weeks but then will be cut off. I wonder if the words "will be cut off" relate to Christ's ascension to heaven. He's no longer able to teach His followers in the personal way He had for the previous years. If "cut off" refers to Jesus's death and going to heaven, then the math starts to get interesting.[11]

It all starts with a declaration to build the temple and getting Jerusalem back in the year 457 BC. Daniel 9 talks about a total of seventy weeks. It's believed that every week is actually seven years, which gives us a total of 490 years. The 490 years begin with a decree to restore and rebuild Jerusalem. Restore means to return the city to the Jews to serve as their capital from which they would rule their whole nation, according to their own laws. The article "Which Decree Began the 490 Years of Daniel 9?" evaluates four Persian decrees:

1. The decree by Cyrus in 538/7 BC allowed the Jews to rebuild Jerusalem but didn't give Jerusalem back to the nation to serve as their national capital.

---

[11] Andries Van Niekerk, "The 490 Years of Daniel 9—Evaluation of the Four Major Interpretations," From Daniel to Revelation, June 20, 2013, https://revelationbyjesuschrist.com/daniel-9-summary/.

2. The decree by Darius I in 520 BC simply confirmed Cyrus's edict.
3. The decree by Artaxerxes I in 457 BC for the first time granted autonomy to Judah, and if we add 483 years to 457 BC, we come to the time of Christ. This is, therefore, the decree referred to in the Daniel 9 prophecy.
4. The second decree by Artaxerxes—in 445/4 BC—simply confirmed his previous decree and was too late to fit the time of Christ.[12]

So 457 BC and Daniel's 483 years bring us to AD 27. Remember that the Roman calendar has no 0 year, and Jesus died in AD 28. This date doesn't line up with what you'll hear from most scholars, but I'll explain it later in the book. Again, the math is going to get interesting. This brings us to the day that Jesus rode a donkey into Jerusalem.[13]

The 490 years begin with a decree to restore and rebuild Jerusalem. Restore means to return the city to the Jews to serve as their capital, from which they would rule their whole nation, according to their own laws.[14]

---

[12] Andries Van Niekerk, "Which Decree Began the 490 Years of Daniel 9?" Revelation by Jesus Christ, April 7, 2018, https://revelationbyjesuschrist.com/decree-to-restore-jerusalem/.

[13] Stephen Dexter, "Prophetic Parallels—Rapture & Tribulation," YouTube video, November 28, 2021, https://www.youtube.com/watch?v=LQKyENfWiis.

[14] RockIslandBooks, "Is the End of Days Prophesied in the First Word of the Bible?" YouTube video, November 21, 2018, 1:05;27, https://www.youtube.com/watch?v=PtATSQx3cjI; thelivingword, "Message for Israel Hidden in Pi," YouTube videos, December 5, 2015, https://www.youtube.com/watch?v=ZKMlfWNH-Bk.

TEN
ASTEROID

"And except those days should be shortened, there should no flesh be saved: but for the elect's sake those days shall be shortened" (Matthew 24:22, KJV).

I looked when He opened the sixth seal, and behold, there was a great earthquake; and the sun became black as sackcloth of hair, and the moon became like blood. And the stars of heaven fell to the earth, as a fig tree drops its late figs when it is shaken by a mighty wind. Then the sky receded as a scroll when it is rolled up, and every mountain and island was moved out of its place. And the kings of the earth, the great men, the rich men, the commanders, the mighty men, every slave and every free man, hid themselves in the caves and in the rocks of the mountains, and said to the mountains and rocks, "Fall on us and hide us from the face of Him who sits on the throne and from the wrath of the Lamb! For the great day of His wrath has come, and who is able to stand?" (Revelation 6:12–17, NKJV)

Then the second angel sounded: And something like a great mountain burning with fire was thrown into the sea,

> and a third of the sea became blood. And a third of the
> living creatures in the sea died, and a third of the ships
> were destroyed. Then the third angel sounded: And a
> great star fell from heaven, burning like a torch, and it
> fell on a third of the rivers and on the springs of water.
> The name of the star is Wormwood. A third of the waters
> became wormwood, and many men died from the water,
> because it was made bitter. (Revelation 8:8–11, NKJV)

IF YOU'RE FAMILIAR with how our little solar system works, you know that the sun is stationary compared to the earth, and the earth rotates every twenty-four hours, which gives us one day and one night. If we take the literal meaning, and the days are going to be shorter, as indicated in Matthew 24:22 that would mean that the earth is going to have to spin faster. I'd like to explore this, just to see what's involved.

So what is going to cause the earth to spin faster? It could possibly be caused by a big enough asteroid that hits the earth near the Equator at a very shallow angle, almost like a glancing blow, so that the speed of the asteroid would actually speed up the earth's rotation. This angle would have to be more than forty-five degrees, as any less than that would result in too much material bouncing off and going back into space. This would cause a major earthquake, as described in Revelation 6:12. Is it possible that all of these verses actually refer to the same event?

TEN: ASTEROID

ASTEROID APOPHIS IS COMING IN 2029

The timing of this event is intriguing. This asteroid is 340 metres, or 1,100 feet across. In terms of mass, you'd need twenty-seven of these asteroids to get one cubic mile. The earth is 260 billion cubic miles. Apophis would cause a crater 1 mile, or 1.6 kilometres wide, and 1,700 feet, or 518 metres deep. But there's no way it could speed up the earth enough to satisfy these verses. Realistically the speed increase is less than one second.

If an asteroid much bigger, say 10 or 20 miles across moves the planet, there will be a couple of side effects to keep in mind. The impact would be so severe that a plow wind of eight hundred kilometres an hour would sweep the earth several times around. Secondly the heat generated from the impact would cause an instantaneous fire that would follow the plow wind and also sweep the earth. No one living on the surface of the planet would survive.

How big of an asteroid would be needed to speed up the rotation of the earth to make a real difference, say a three-hour shorter day? It would be relative to the speed, but it would most likely be bigger than twenty miles across.

So how does the earth speed up to satisfy these verses? A fast-moving object that hits the surface doesn't seem to fit, so does that leave a large, slow-moving object? We're still faced with the problem that if it hits the earth and causes the planet's rotation to change, it's going to cause too much damage to the surface of the earth. How about a really big, highly magnetic planet that doesn't hit the surface but comes close enough to affect the rotation. I've found at least twenty different websites that deal with this, only to go back a week later to find the website gone.

WHERE ARE WE?

"And if the Lord had not cut short the days, no human being would be saved. But for the sake of the elect, whom he chose, he shortened the days" (Mark 13:20, ESV).[15]

---

[15] The 700 Club, "The Wormwood Prophecy," YouTube video, March 9, 2020, 9:00, https://www.youtube.com/watch?v=xEgzqq9YMLU; Dexter, "Prophetic Parallels—Rapture & Tribulation."

THE AFTER DATE

IF WE COULD narrow down when the tribulation will occur, we'd be left with an idea of when the Rapture will take place. Let's start by examining different translations of Hosea 6:2.

> After two days he will revive us; on the third day he will restore us, that we may live in his presence. (NIV)

> After two days he will revive us; on the third day he will raise us up, that we may live before him. (ESV)

> After two days will he revive us: in the third day he will raise us up, and we shall live in his sight. (KJV)

> He will revive us after two days; He will raise us up on the third day, That we may live before Him. (NASB)

> In just a short time he will restore us, so that we may live in his presence (NLT).

> He will revive us after two days, and on the third day he will raise us up so we can live in his presence. (CSB)

WHERE ARE WE?

Many commentaries take the first part of this verse and conclude that it's a reference to Jesus dying, being buried for two days, then rising on the third day. But you have to read the entire verse. From what I read, this theory isn't supported.

Hosea 6:2 says that He will revive us after two days. It's believed that a day is interchangeable with a thousand years on the earth.

"And this one thing let not be unobserved by you, beloved, that one day with the Lord [is] as a thousand years, and a thousand years as one day" (2 Peter 3:8, YLT). So does this mean we will be revived after two thousand years? Presently, it's believed that these years form the gap in Daniel's seventy-weeks prophecy. The gap began at the time of Jesus's death or ascension into heaven.

If this is so, when did Jesus die? This isn't directly addressed in the Bible. How old did Jesus get? Approximately thirty-three years. When was he born? If we can pinpoint when He was born, we'll be able to know when he died.

The first clue can be found in Luke 2:8: *"And there were in the same country shepherds abiding in the field, keeping watch over their flock by night"* (KJV). Around fifty years ago, I first heard this verse in a Christmas program. A still, small voice said to me: "There's more to this verse." The tone of the voice seemed to imply that people don't understand.

After a minute, I started asking myself if it had been a message from an angel or someone sitting behind me. I needed to make sure before anyone behind me moved. So I turned around and looked at the people. They looked at me, clearly wondering why I was looking at them. I must have recognized them, because I remember thinking

ELEVEN: THE AFTER DATE

that the voice I'd heard didn't sound like any of them. I looked up and down the bench, but there was no one sitting there with a voice that matched what I'd heard. I turned around and thought to myself, *Well, that was interesting. Now what? I am but a child. What can I do? Who's going to listen to me?*

Over the years, I forgot about this event. Then one day I was researching shepherds in Bethlehem, reading about when they're in the field and when they're not, and then I remembered those words I'd heard. It had taken over fifty years to find what was hidden. Why doesn't this verse jump out at us? It's because most who read this aren't shepherds.

First, we need to ask why the shepherds were in the field. Two thousand years ago, an abundance of animals thought of sheep as food; therefore, it was dangerous to keep sheep in an open field. Shepherds wouldn't take them out there unless there was a very good reason. In my research, I learned that shepherds in Bethlehem at that time would take their sheep into the field from one month to six months, but generally it was less than two months. Why? The sheep are in the fields to eat the fresh green growth of spring.

Bethlehem is in the Northern Hemisphere, so summer lands in July and winter in December. The shepherds would not go out in December. It would have been too cold and there wouldn't have been anything for the sheep to eat.

In Vancouver, Canada, spring growth can start in February. In Saskatchewan, it's more likely to come in May. On the hills of Bethlehem, it occurs in March or April. Perhaps we can narrow it down even further, pegging it between March 10 and April 10.

WHERE ARE WE?

As for the year of Jesus's birth, we can start by looking at Matthew 2:16–19. This passage tells the story of Herod meeting the wise men and getting upset when they didn't come back after finding Jesus. It's important to note here that there was a time period when Jesus and Herod were alive at the same time. Herod then ordered the death of all children around the age of two.

Herod died in 4 BC. Even if Herod had died the very next week after giving this order, Jesus's birth year would range from 5 to 7 BC. Some people are shocked to learn that Herod died in 4 BC. There is no way that Jesus was born at year 0, lived thirty-four years, and died in 34 AD.

There are some reports that after Herod ordered the death of God's son, his mind deteriorated before his death. If we backtrack from his death in 4 BC to when he had a sound mind while meeting with the wise men, that could take us to a year earlier. That would put the meeting in 5 BC. This means that Jesus was probably born in the middle of the two-year declaration against the Hebrew boys. This would put the birth of Jesus around 6 BC.

One needs to remember that Herod had a son, and his son was also named Herod. Helpfully, though, the Bible mentions numerous political leaders as well as the respective positions they held at the time. The years of these leaders' influence may not be documented in the Bible, but they are well-documented in other sources.

If one takes into account each person and looks for a year in which all were in power at the same time, the conclusion will be that Jesus was born in approximately 6 BC. Everet Harrison in his book *A Short Life of Christ* refers to a census in 8 BC. The

ELEVEN: THE AFTER DATE

execution of the census may have been delayed, putting the birth of Christ in 6 BC. Herod died in 4 BC.[16]

So why do we celebrate Christ's birth on December 25? There are some hints in Matthew 2:5. Herod was told where Jesus was to be born (Matthew 2:7) and then he inquired as to when the star of Bethlehem first appeared (Matthew 2:13). That's when Herod decided to destroy the child (Matthew 2:16). Based on information from the wise men, he had all male children with a recorded birthday close to Jesus's killed. So there was a definite motive to change the date. Wouldn't the people of that time who knew Jesus was special do everything in their power to protect Him? We may never know why the date was changed, but most scholars agree that Christ was not born in December. Johnathan Cahn has an interesting video that provides some insight into the timeline.[17]

In the video cited above, the date of Christ's birth is revealed as March 20, 6 BC. They mention three main points: sheep are only in the field from March to August, shepherds only watch the sheep at night during lambing season (March and April), and according to Exodus 12:3, a sacrificial lamb must be a year old at Passover, meaning it had to be born in spring.

Herod reigned from 37 to 4 BC, and he died in March or April, 4 BC. His son, Herod Archelaus reigned from 4 BC to AD 6. He was removed by the Roman Emperor Augustus when the Judaean province was formed under direct Roman rule at the time of the census. So Herod's son ruled for nine years.

---

[16] Everet Harrison, *A Short Life of Christ* (Grand Rapids, MI: Wm. B. Eerdmans Publishing Co., 1968), 38.

[17] Bruce Avilla, "When Was Jesus Really Born?" YouTube video, December 13, 2014, 27:20, https://www.youtube.com/watch?v=ptIsXtTf6n0.

WHERE ARE WE?

Herod's decree meant that Joseph, Mary, and Jesus fled for Egypt when Jesus was less than two years old. They would have moved around in Egypt from spot to stop every six months. They returned to Nazareth after three years, making Jesus at most five years old. Matthew 2:19–22 spells it out clearly.

> After Herod died, an angel of the Lord appeared in a dream to Joseph in Egypt and said, "Get up, take the child and his mother and go to the land of Israel, for those who were trying to take the child's life are dead." So he got up, took the child and his mother and went to the land of Israel. But when he heard that Archelaus was reigning in Judea in place of his father Herod, he was afraid to go there. Having been warned in a dream, he withdrew to the district of Galilee.

Herod Archelaus was in power until AD 6 and died in AD 18. Joseph, Mary, and Jesus were only in Egypt for two years.[18]

Jesus was born during a census taken in 7 BC to 6 BC. The census was called in 8 BC but might have been delayed, as people like Mary and Joesph needed time to travel.

The time-line for Herod the Great works better. If the star appeared at the time of the conception, and the wise men travelled for one year, they would have arrived when Jesus was three months old, around 6 BC. Herod the Great died in April of 4 BC. God then

---

[18] Christopher R. Smith, "How Long Did Jesus Live in Egypt?" Good Question, July 10, 2014, https://goodquestionblog.com/2014/07/10/how-long-did-jesus-live-in-egypt/.

ELEVEN: THE AFTER DATE

tells Joseph to come back with his family, and they return in the spring of 3 BC.

The following are eleven important people, but none of them die at the right time to be considered important in the timeline of Jesus's return from Egypt.

Herod Antipas was a first-century ruler of Galilee and Perea, who bore the title of tetrarch. He is referred to as both "Herod the Tetrarch" and "King Herod" in the New Testament, although he never held the title of king. He was a son of Herod the Great and a grandson of Antipater the Idumaean. In AD 39, Antipas was accused by his nephew Agrippa I of conspiracy against the Roman emperor Caligula, who sent him into exile in Gaul, according to Josephus. Accompanied there by Herodias, he died at an unknown date, but obviously it was after AD 39.

Herod Agrippa, also known as Herod II or Agrippa I, was a King of Judea from AD 41 to 44. He was the last ruler with the royal title to reign over Judea, and he was the father of Herod Agrippa II, the last king from the Herodian dynasty. He was born in 11 BC and died in AD 44 AD in Caesarea National Park, Caesarea, Israel.

Herod Archelaus was ethnarch of Samaria, Judea, and Idumea, including the cities Caesarea and Jaffa, for a period of nine years. He was removed by Roman emperor Augustus when the Judaean province was formed under direct Roman rule, at the time of the census of Quirinius. He was born in 23 BC and died in AD 18 in Gaul.

Herod II was the son of Herod the Great and Mariamne II, the daughter of Simon Boethus, the High Priest. For a brief period he was his father's heir apparent, but Herod I removed him from succession in his will. He was born in 27 BC and died in AD 33.

Herod Agrippa II, officially named Marcus Julius Agrippa and sometimes shortened to Agrippa, was the last ruler from the Herodian dynasty, reigning over territories outside of Judea as a Roman client. He was born in AD 27 in Rome and died in AD 100 in Rome.

Philip the Tetrarch, sometimes called Herod Philip II by modern writers, son of Herod the Great and his fifth wife, Cleopatra of Jerusalem, ruled over the northeast part of his father's kingdom between 4 BC and AD 34, when he died in Bethsaida.

Aristobulus IV was a prince of Judea from the Herodian dynasty. He was married to his cousin, Berenice, daughter of Costobarus and Salome I. He was the son of Herod the Great and his second wife, Mariamne I, the last of the Hasmoneans, and was thus a descendant of the Hasmonean Dynasty. He was born in 31 BC and died in 7 BC in Samaria.

Antipater II was Herod the Great's first-born son, his only child by his first wife, Doris. He was named after his paternal grandfather Antipater the Idumaean. He and his mother were exiled after Herod divorced her between 43 BC and 40 BC to marry Mariamne I. He was born in 46 BC and died in 4 BC in Jerusalem.

Pheroras, probably born in Marissa, was the youngest son of Antipater I and his wife Cypros, and younger brother of Herod the Great. His first marriage was to a sister of Mariamne I. The marriage was allegedly arranged by Herod. He was born in Maresha, Israel and died in 5 BC in Perea.

ELEVEN: THE AFTER DATE

Alexander, son of Herod, was born about 35 BC and died around 7 BC. His mother was the Hasmonean princess Mariamne. He was born in 35 BC and died in 7 BC in Samaria.

During my research, I didn't find a "Herod" or an important relative who died between the years AD 1 and AD 5 to support the idea that Jesus was born in year "0." Tiberius Caesar Augustus was born on November 16, 42 BC and died on March 16, AD 37. Pontius Pilate was governor of Judaea from AD 26 to 36. Caiaphas was a high priest for eighteen years (AD 18 to 36).

The angel said to Joseph, *"Get up, take the child and his mother and go to the land of Israel, for those who were trying to take the child's life are dead"* (Matthew 2:20). Who are "those" in this verse?

Antipater II, Herod's first-born son, was killed by Herod. Herod wanted to kill God's son, but God allowed his mind to fail to such a state that he killed his own son.

Malthace was one of Herod the Great's wives and the mother by Herod of Herod Antipas, Archelaus, and a daughter, Olympias. She died in 4 BC at Rome while her sons were disputing the will of their father before Emperor Augustus. If we look at Matthew 2:19 along with verse 20, we'll gain a different perspective on "those" who must have died at almost the same time: *"After Herod died, an angel of the Lord appeared in a dream to Joseph in Egypt and said, "Get up, take the child and his mother and go to the land of Israel, for those who were trying to take the child's life are dead."* There is nothing more protective than the bond between the mother and her children. To add to this, Malthace's welfare depended on one of her sons remaining in power. The threat of someone else being a future king was a threat to her children as well as to her. If Jesus were

WHERE ARE WE?

to live, Malthace needed to die. The army was ultimately loyal to Herod, and upon his death, its loyalties split, as there doesn't seem to be information on major army decisions after the death of Herod.

Instead of zeroing in on one direction, at times I've tried to explore all possibilities and all the glitches and intricacies of any formula. Here are two of them.

Truthbook pegs Jesus's birthday at August 21, 7 BC.[19]

We also need to keep in mind that only in the last century has it become more common for businesses and organizations to start their calendar years on the day the business started and not follow a typical January to December year. The further back in time you go, the more you will find that a year is considered to be January to December.

So if a prophecy was made in February and it said "wait one year and it will occur in spring," this would mean you should wait until January, then one year, then until spring. So what we first thought was one year and three months could be interpreted as two years and three months.

The birthdate needs to be in spring to satisfy the sheep being in the field. So let's go back to March 20, 6 BC, and try to determine the date of Christ's death. If you add thirty-three years to six you get the spring of AD 27, right? Wrong. The Roman calendar doesn't have a 0. When the Romans designed the calendar, they didn't have a number for 0, so they purposely designed a calendar with

---

[19] Chris M. Halvorson, "When Is Jesus' Birthday?" Truthbook, accessed June 6, 2025, https://truthbook.com/jesus/when-is-jesus-birthday/?gclid=CjwKCAiA3L6PBhBvEi-wAINIJ9DCoYnPm2oSk--gCdR9WyDhlwpove_nSbO7p-gpoxLIPyuSSqoIvfhoCO9U-QAvD_BwE.

ELEVEN: THE AFTER DATE

no 0. This means if you start at 6 BC and add six years, you arrive at AD 1. So Jesus's life of thirty-three years brings you to AD 28.

"Now from the sixth hour until the ninth hour there was darkness over all the land" (Matthew 27:45, KJV). Many people conclude that there must have been a solar eclipse, and then they research what years are compatible with a solar eclipse over that area. There's a big problem with this conclusion. Jesus was crucified during Passover (Matthew 26:2). What is Passover? To understand this, we need to go back to the time of Ramesses II in 1279 BC to 1212 BC and particularly focus on the ten plagues of Egypt. The last plague was the killing of the first-born son. To escape this plague, the Hebrews were to sacrifice an unblemished lamb and put the blood on the top of the door frame of their houses. At night, God's angel would see the blood and pass over their house. Those with the blood escaped the plague, and then God instituted the annual Passover meal to commemorate this event.

After this plague, Pharaoh allowed the Hebrew people to leave Egypt. Exodus 12:40 tells us that the Hebrews had lived in Egypt 430 years. Freedom after 430 years of slavery was a real event to celebrate. In Exodus 12:6, God commands the people to prepare the lamb on the fourteenth day of the month, but the actual date of the Passover is the fifteenth. The Hebrew calendar is different from the Roman calendar. The Hebrew calendar, or Jewish calendar, follows the stages of the moon, so on the fifteenth of their first month, they celebrate the Passover.

Jesus was crucified during Passover. As a Jew, he Had come to Jerusalem for the event. But is that just a coincidence? Did Jesus just happen to die during Passover? The biblical answer is no.

WHERE ARE WE?

The reason He came to Jerusalem that final time wasn't just to celebrate Passover but to become our Passover.

Passover takes place during the full moon, meaning the moon is at the exact opposite side of the earth, where you would need it to support a solar eclipse. Both holidays are supposed to fall on, or near, a full moon in the spring. Passover always begins on the fifteenth day of the Hebrew month of Nisan. Because the Hebrew months are pegged directly to the lunar cycle, the fifteenth day of Nisan always falls on a full moon.[20]

This leaves a problem that we can't explain. What caused the darkness over the land in Matthew 27:45? The only real answer is that if God can create planet Earth, He can also create some asteroid or rogue planet to block out the sun for a few hours. Such a body coming that close to earth would cause other side effects, like earthquakes.

> Then, behold, the veil of the temple was torn in two from top to bottom; and the earth quaked, and the rocks were split, and the graves were opened; and many bodies of the saints who had fallen asleep were raised; and coming out of the graves after His resurrection, they went into the holy city and appeared to many. So when the centurion and those with him, who were guarding Jesus, saw the earthquake and the things that had happened, they feared greatly, saying, "Truly this was the Son of God!" (Matthew 27:51–54, NKJV)

---

[20] Jake Parks, "Understanding the Phases of the Moon," Astronomy, August 30, 2023, https://www.astronomy.com/observing/understanding-the-phases-of-the-moon/.

ELEVEN: THE AFTER DATE

I found an article on the internet that presents an interesting concept.

> Ryan Maderak ... has a different take. Scientifically, yes, the moon would have been on the wrong side of Earth at Passover, making a solar eclipse during the crucifixion impossible .... Maderak said, "If God is omnipotent, then he has sort of a little, shall we say, a little leeway to override the laws of physics ... "What I'm getting at here: Miraculous occurrences are just that."[21]

Returning to Hosea 6:2, I've read a number of articles on the internet about this passage, and the consensus among different theologians is that we must wait for this date to pass. Once it does pass, something will happen shortly afterwards. Adding Daniel's two-thousand-year gap to the year April AD 28 brings us to a date after Easter—April 17, 2028.

I think there's something behind the two-thousand-year gap. In Exodus, we read about Moses leading God's people through the desert to the Promised Land. Moses sent spies to see the Promised Land. The people occupying the land were huge in comparison to the Israelites. The Israelites didn't trust God and were too scared to continue, so Moses had to lead them around in the desert for forty years until all the original Israelites had died so that their children could enter the Promised Land.

---

[21] Eric Adler, "Was Jesus Crucified During a Solar Eclipse? NASA Shows One Occurred in 33 A.D.," *The Kansas City Star*, August 7, 2017, https://www.kansascity.com/news/local/article165869047.html.

WHERE ARE WE?

Fast forward to the time of Jesus's death. It wasn't the government pushing for Jesus' crucifixion but the common people—the people Jesus had talked to, witnessed to, and healed. These were the people who pushed for God's son's, Jesus's, death. Is it possible that this was not the original plan and that God decided to punish the people by ramping up the 40 year wait time to 40 jubilee years?

God decided to punish these people by pushing a possible wait time of forty years for the rapture to occur to a forty jubilee-year wait time. A jubilee year occurs once every fifty years. I believe there's something to this, but it would require more research.

THE BEFORE DATE

"TRULY I TELL you, this generation will certainly not pass away until all these things have happened" (Matthew 24:34). Luke also recorded the lesson of the fig tree.

> And he spake to them a parable; Behold the fig tree, and all the trees; When they now shoot forth, ye see and know of your own selves that summer is now nigh at hand. So likewise ye, when ye see these things come to pass, know ye that the kingdom of God is nigh at hand. Verily I say unto you, This generation shall not pass away, till all be fulfilled. Heaven and earth shall pass away: but my words shall not pass away. (Luke 21:29–33, KJV; see also Matthew 24:32–35; Mark 13:28–31)

It's interesting that the parable starts with the image of a tree. Your relatives and ancestors are often referred to as your family tree. If someone dies childless, that branch ends. Having a "tree shoot forth" means new hope for the entire tree.

Does this mean the start date of this generation is when Israel became a nation on May 14, 1948? What is a generation? There are many references to a "generation" in the Bible, and it ranges from 40 to 110 years, depending on situations and lifestyles. Psalm

WHERE ARE WE?

90:10 describes a generation in terms we use today: *"The days of our lives are seventy years; And if by reason of strength they are eighty years, Yet their boast is only labor and sorrow; For it is soon cut off, and we fly away"* (KJV). "By reason of strength" could be related to what has happened in the last eighty years: hot and cold running water, central heating systems, health care/medication availability.

The last part of the verse, though, seems rather odd, but if we put it in the context of the last eighty years out of a seven-thousand-year time period of human life on earth—and if we also think of this verse summing up the last five thousand years—then it makes sense. The last part of the verse seems to imply that this length of a generation refers to a generation that's alive right before the Rapture/Tribulation time period.

The book of Psalms was written over quite a length of time. Psalm 90 was written around 1400 BC. Did eighty years mean the same then as it does today? Not exactly. Obituaries don't just say that someone was eighty years old. They tell us how old the person was in years, months, and days. When considering things historically, you need to look at the culture and the way of thinking. They didn't count years, months, and days back then. They were either eighty or eighty-one (but after their eighty-first birthday). So eighty years and eleven months and twenty-five days was still a plain, simple eighty. This means that May 14, 1948, plus a generation of eighty years, is 2028—sometime before May 14, 2028 becomes May 13, 2029.

TWELVE: THE BEFORE DATE

A couple of interesting notes about the dates:

- The after-date formula starts 2,500 years ago, and the before-date starts 75 years ago.
- The two formulas are not a thousand years apart.
- The dates are in the right order—after April 17, 2028 but before May 14, 2028 and possibly stretched to May 13, 2029.

I thought about this for a while and remembered a conversation (one-sided) I had with the Lord many years ago, probably back when I was a teenager. I had heard of the verse that tells us that no one knows the day or the hour, so I read it over and thought about it. Then I made a decision: "Lord, I don't want to know the hour. I'd be more than happy to know the month." I never could have imagined where that would lead.

In Jewish tradition, the exact date of a wedding is decided by the father of the bride. This is a parallel to the Rapture. In this wedding, we know it's getting close, but at this moment in time, we don't have the information to accurately determine the date of the Rapture.

Side note: On April 13, 2029, Apophis will pass less than 20,000 miles (32,000 kilometres) from our planet's surface—closer than the distance of geosynchronous satellites. During that 2029 close approach, Apophis will be visible to observers on the ground in the Eastern Hemisphere without the aid of a telescope or binoculars. It's also an unprecedented opportunity for astronomers to get a close-up view of a solar system relic that's now just

WHERE ARE WE?

a scientific curiosity and not an immediate hazard to our planet. Apophis is named for the demon serpent who personified evil and chaos in ancient Egyptian mythology. Could this signal the evil and chaos that is coming to this world, or could this just be another coincidence?

THIRTEEN
AI

MORE THAN ONE thousand technology leaders and researchers, including Elon Musk, have urged artificial intelligence labs to pause development of the most advanced systems, warning in an open letter that AI tools present "profound risks to society and humanity."[22]

AI developers are "locked in an out-of-control race to develop and deploy ever more powerful digital minds that no one—not even their creators—can understand, predict or reliably control,"[23] according to the letter, which the nonprofit Future of Life Institute released on Wednesday.

What is Elon Musk's opinion on artificial intelligence? Unless we build in safeguards, Musk argued, artificial-intelligence-systems might replace humans, making our species irrelevant or even extinct.

In 2023, Musk predicted that superintelligence, or AI that is smarter than humans, will arrive in five or six years. Musk co-founded OpenAI, the company behind ChatGPT, in 2015, but stepped down from the company's board in 2018. Microsoft is an investor in OpenAI. This puts arrival date in 2028 so does this

---

[22] "Pause Giant AI Experiments: An Open Letter," Future of Life, accessed June 6, 2025, https://futureoflife.org/open-letter/pause-giant-ai-experiments/.
[23] Ibid.

mean that the antichrist is part AI or is this just another coincidence?[24]

Have you ever noticed that after talking about something you get ads on that subject in your social media feed? Android phones have built-in factory programming to listen to you, monitor your conversations, and relay that information to the advertisers. Want to turn it off? Check out the Appendix.

---

[24] Sarah Fortinsky, "Musk Predicts 'Digital Superintelligence' Will Exist in 5–6 Years," The Hill, July 12, 2023, https://thehill.com/policy/technology/4094606-musk-predicts-digital-superintelligence-will-exist-in-5-6-years/.

FOURTEEN
THE THIRD TEMPLE

CORNERSTONES

A GROUP CALLED "The Temple Mount Faithful," led by Gershom Salomon, has prepared the cornerstones for a new Temple using tools to cut diamond rather than steel, so as to conform with the biblical injunction that no metal tool be used in the construction of the Temple—an edifice of peace.[25]

STONES FOR THE ALTAR

In 2010, uncut stones were collected from the Dead Sea for the construction of the Temple altar. Such pristine stones are believed to fulfill the injunction that such building material be free from contact with metal tools. The instruments for use in the daily rituals have all been made and are actually on display for the public to see.[26]

---

[25] Israel's Priests Prepare for the Third Temple," The Messianic Prophecy Bible Project, accessed June 6, 2025, https://free.messianicbible.com/feature/israels-priests-prepare-third-temple/; "The Temple Vessels Are Ready for the Rebuilding of Jerusalem's Third Temple," The Messianic Prophecy Bible Project, accessed June 6, 2025, https://free.messianicbible.com/feature/the-temple-vessels-are-ready-for-the-rebuilding-of-jerusalems-third-temple/.

[26] Ibid.

WHERE ARE WE?

THE ANIMALS FOR SLAUGHTER

In September 2022, five red heifers were selected in Texas and shipped to Israel for sacrifice in the third temple.[27]

I have read in the past that all the supplies needed for the third temple have been bought and are sitting in storage waiting for the right moment to build it. It will take three to four years to build. Is it just another coincidence that the first half of the tribulation is three and a half years of peace?

---

[27] "The Red Heifer Prophecy," YouTube Shorts, March 30, 2024, https://www.youtube.com/shorts/IrEheqEMvTU.

FIFTEEN
FIFTY REASONS WHY THE RAPTURE IS CLOSE

1. Increasing instability of nature (Luke 21:11)
2. Increasing lawlessness and violence (Matthew 24:12)
3. Increasing immorality (Matthew 24:37)
4. Increasing materialism (2 Timothy 3:2)
5. Increasing hedonism (2 Timothy 3:4)
6. Increasing influence of humanism (2 Timothy 3:2)
7. Depraved entertainment (2 Timothy 3:4)
8. Calling evil good and good evil (2 Timothy 3:3)
9. Increasing use of drugs (2 Timothy 3:2)
10. Increasing blasphemy (2 Timothy 3:2)
11. Increasing paganism (2 Timothy 3:1–4)
12. Increasing despair (2 Timothy 3:1)
13. Increasing knowledge (Daniel 12:4)
14. Increasing travel (Daniel 12:4)
15. Signs in the heavens (Luke 21:11, 25)
16. Explosion of cults (Matthew 24:11)
17. Proliferation of false Christs (Matthew 24:5)
18. Increasing apostasy in the Church (2 Timothy 4:3–5)
19. Increasing attacks on Jesus (Romans 1:18)
20. Increasing attacks on the Bible (Romans 1:18)
21. Increasing persecution of Christians (Matthew 24:9)

22. Increasing occultism (1 Timothy 4:1)
23. Wars and rumours of wars (Matthew 24:6)
24. Weapons of mass destruction (Luke 21:26)
25. Computer technology (Revelation 13:7)
26. Television (Revelation 11:8–9)
27. Satellite technology (Revelation 13:7, 11:9)
28. Virtual reality (Revelation 13:14–15)
29. Medical technology (Revelation 9:16)
30. Population explosion (Revelation 9:16)
31. Unification of Europe (Daniel 2, 7)
32. Far Eastern military powers
33. Movement toward world government
34. Regathering of the Jews (Isaiah 11:10–12)
35. Re-establishment of Israel (Isaiah 66:7–8)
36. Re-claiming of the land of Israel (Ezekiel 36:34–35)
37. Revival of biblical Hebrew (Zephaniah 3:6)
38. Re-occupation of Jerusalem (Luke 21:24)
39. Resurgence of the Israeli military (Zechariah 12:6)
40. Re-focusing of world politics on Jerusalem (Zechariah 12:3)
41. Russian threat to Israel (Ezekiel 38, 39)
42. Arab threat to Israel (Ezekiel 35, 36)
43. Denial of the second coming (2 Peter 3:3–4)
44. Denial of creation by God (Romans 1:18–22)
45. Outpouring of the Holy Spirit (Joel 2:28–29)
46. Translation of the Bible into many languages (Matthew 24:14)
47. Preaching of the gospel worldwide (Matthew 24:14)

FIFTEEN: FIFTY REASONS WHY THE RAPTURE IS CLOSE

48. Establishment of Messianic Judaism (Isaiah 40:3–5)
49. The revival of David's worship (Amos 9:11)
50. The understanding of biblical prophecy (Daniel 2:8–9)[28]

---

[28] Compass International, "50 Reasons Rapture's Close—Dave Reagan," YouTube Video, April 13, 2022, 43:21, https://www.youtube.com/watch?v=dV_qea_jM8Q.

AUTHORS NOTE

MORE INFORMATION ON the Rapture is coming out so fast that I can't seem to keep up with it, but the Lord has encouraged me to finish the book. If I wait until I think I have all the information, this book will never get finished. The information I'm finding now will have to wait for Book Two.

APPENDIX

HOW TO TURN off your Android phone so it doesn't listen to you:
    Go to main settings.
    Scroll to Google and tap on it.
    Tap on "All Services."
    Scroll down to "Privacy and Security."
    Tap on "Personalize Using Shared Data."
    Disable all items on the list that pop up.
    Tap "Back" on top left corner of screen.
    Go to "Privacy and Security."
    Tap on "Usage and Diagnostics" and turn it off.
    Go back to "Privacy and Security."
    Tap on "Ads."
    Scroll down to find "Reset Advertising ID" and tap on it.
    Tap on "Confirm."
    Tap on "Delete Advertising ID."
    Tap again on the popup to delete.[29]

---

[29] Useful Things, "Your Android Phone Tracking You and Listening. TURN THIS OFF," YouTube video, August 1, 2024, 3:41, https://www.youtube.com/watch?v=Es_uQA-QkNXo.

www.ingramcontent.com/pod-product-compliance
Lightning Source LLC
Chambersburg PA
CBHW032020040426
42448CB00006B/684